Camper Van
& Camping
Cookbook

igloobooks

Published in 2013
by Igloo Books Ltd
Cottage Farm
Sywell
NN6 0BJ
www.igloobooks.com

HUN001 0213
2 4 6 8 10 9 7 5 3 1
ISBN 978-1-78197-171-0

Food photographyand recipe development: Photocuisine UK

Printed and manufactured in China

Camper Van & Camping
Cookbook

Contents

Breakfast 6

Lunch 24

Starters & Sides 46

Mains 64

Desserts 106

Breakfast

Porridge with Maple Syrup

INGREDIENTS

500 ml / 1 pint / 2 cups milk or water
OR half and half

60 g / 2½ oz / ¼ cup medium oatmeal
1 tsp salt

To serve:
maple syrup
dark brown sugar
4 tbsp single cream

METHOD

Heat the milk and/or water in a pan until almost boiling.

Whisk in the oatmeal a little at a time until the mixture returns to the boil.

Reduce the heat, cover the pan and leave to cook very gently for 10 minutes, stirring occasionally to prevent sticking.

Whisk in the salt, then leave to cook very gently for 10-15 minutes more, again stirring occasionally.

Serve with the syrup and / or sugar and 2 tbsp of cream poured over the top.

serves **2**

preparation time **5** mins

cooking time **25** mins

Poached Eggs and Ham on Toasted Brioche

INGREDIENTS

150 ml / 5 fl. oz / ⅔ cup whipping cream
1 bunch chives, finely chopped
4 eggs
4 thick slices ham
4 brioche rolls
30 g / 1 oz butter

METHOD

Whisk the cream to soft peak, then stir through the chives.

Poach the eggs in boiling water for about 3 minutes for a runny yolk. Remove and place on kitchen paper and leave to drain.

Cut the brioche rolls in half horizontally and lightly toast the cut sides, then butter.

Place the brioche on a plate and lay over the slices of ham.

Top with the poached eggs and serve the chive cream alongside.

serves
4

preparation time
10 mins

cooking time
5 mins

French Toast with Chocolate

INGREDIENTS

1 thick slice of white bread per person
2 eggs, beaten
300 ml / 10 fl. oz / 1¼ cups full fat milk
OR single cream

1 tsp vanilla extract
½ tsp ground cinnamon
1 jar chocolate hazelnut spread (200g)
100 ml / 3½ fl. oz / ½ cup double cream
2 tbsp vegetable oil
sea salt (optional)

METHOD

Cut the bread into triangles.

Whisk together the eggs, milk, vanilla and cinnamon and pour into a bowl.

Lay the bread into the mixture, soaking it thoroughly for a few minutes.

Meanwhile add the chocolate hazelnut spread and cream to a small pan and heat very gently, stirring occasionally until melted and smooth.

Heat the oil in a pan and gently fry the bread triangles 2 at a time until golden and crisp on each side.

Serve with the chocolate sauce and a scant sprinkling of sea salt.

serves
4

preparation time
15
mins

cooking time
10
mins

Herby Scrambled Eggs

INGREDIENTS

6 eggs
40 g / 1 oz / ¼ cup butter
6 tsp double cream
½ bunch parsley, finely chopped
½ bunch chervil or tarragon, finely chopped
½ red pepper, finely diced
100 g / 3½ oz smoked salmon, finely chopped
salt and pepper

hot buttered toast, to serve

METHOD

Crack the eggs into a bowl and beat lightly.

Heat most of the butter in a pan until foaming, then stir in the eggs.

Cook gently, stirring thoroughly with a wooden spoon moving the eggs around the pan until lightly cooked with some liquid egg still left.

Add the peppers and smoked salmon. Stir in the cream, herbs and season. Serve immediately with toast.

serves **4**

preparation time **5** mins

cooking time **8** mins

Pancakes with Summer Berries

INGREDIENTS

225 g / 8 oz / 1 cup plain flour
2 tsp baking powder
1 tsp caster sugar
pinch salt
300 ml / 10 fl. oz / 1¼ cups milk
2 eggs
1 tsp vanilla extract
vegetable oil

mixed berries such as blueberries,
raspberries and strawberries
maple syrup

METHOD

Mix together the flour, baking powder, sugar and salt in a bowl.

Whisk together the milk, eggs and vanilla extract.

Mix the wet ingredients into the dry ingredients to a thick smooth batter then leave to rest for 15 minutes.

Heat a thin film of vegetable oil in the pan and add large dollops of batter to the pan to make circles around 5cm across. Cook until they bubble on top, then turn over and cook for another 1-2 minutes.

Remove from the pan and keep warm while you make the rest.

Serve hot with the berries and syrup.

makes **16**

preparation time **25** mins

cooking time **20** mins

The Full English

INGREDIENTS

vegetable oil
4 sausages
4 rashers back bacon, preferably smoked
10 cherry tomatoes
2 field mushrooms, thickly sliced
2 eggs

METHOD

Heat 3 tbsp vegetable oil in a large frying pan and add the sausages. Cook over a low heat until golden and sticky on all sides, turning occasionally – about 15 minutes.

Turn the heat up a bit and add the bacon to the pan, turning once when the fat is crisp and golden.

Add the tomatoes and mushrooms and leave to cook for 5 minutes, then turn and cook for 2–3 more minutes.

Make a space for the eggs and crack the eggs into the pan. Cover with a lid and leave for 4-5 minutes or until the egg is cooked to your liking.

You can try to slide this out onto the plate in one go or divide into portions with a spatula.

Serve with hot buttered toast.

serves **2**

preparation time **5** mins

cooking time **30** mins

Muesli with Yoghurt

INGREDIENTS

200 g / 7 oz / ¾ cup jumbo porridge oats
1 heaped tbsp bran flakes
3 heaped tbsp rye flakes
2 tbsp hazelnuts, lightly crushed
2 tbsp pumpkin seeds
2 tbsp flaked almonds
2 tbsp sultanas
2 tbsp vegetable or groundnut oil
2 tbsp each mixed dried fruit, such as
apricots, figs or chopped prunes

natural yoghurt and fresh fruit to serve

METHOD

Spread the oats, flakes, nuts and seeds on a plate and toss with the oil until coated.

Heat a large pan over medium heat and toast the muesli in batches for about 7-10 minutes, turning once with a spatula, until lightly golden.

Leave to cool then mix with the dried fruit.

Serve with natural yoghurt and fresh fruit.

serves
4

preparation time
5
mins

cooking time
10
mins

Cheese and Ham Croissant

INGREDIENTS

2 croissants
2 thick slices ham
1 tomato, thickly sliced
60 g / 2 oz / ¼ cup grated cheese

METHOD

Slice the croissants in half horizontally.

Heat the butter in a lidded pan over a medium heat until sizzling then lay in the ham slices.

Top with a couple of tomato slices, then the grated cheese. Place the lid on and cook until the cheese has melted.

Using a spatula, scoop onto the bottom half of the croissant and serve.

serves **2**

preparation time **5** mins

cooking time **6** mins

Lunch

Pasta Salad

INGREDIENTS

320 g / 11 oz / 1¼ cups pasta shapes, such as fusilli or farfalle

2 tbsp olive oil
1 courgette (zucchini), diced
4 tbsp extra virgin olive oil
2 tbsp red wine vinegar
pinch chilli flakes
12 ripe cherry tomatoes, quartered
salt and pepper
1 can tuna, drained
1 bunch basil

METHOD

Cook the pasta in boiling salted water according to packet instructions. Drain, toss with a little oil to prevent sticking and leave to cool.

Meanwhile heat the oil in a pan and sauté the courgette dice until golden and tender. Remove to kitchen paper and drain.

In a bowl whisk the extra virgin oil and vinegar to form an emulsion, season and add the chilli flakes then toss in the tomatoes to macerate.

To compose the salad, mix the pasta gently with the tuna, courgettes and tomatoes in their dressing. Tear up the basil leaves and serve.

serves **4**

preparation time **15** mins

cooking time **11** mins

Lentil Soup
with Hazelnuts

INGREDIENTS

2 tbsp olive oil
1 onion, peeled and finely chopped
2 carrots, peeled and diced
2 sticks celery, finely chopped
1 clove of garlic, finely chopped
175 g / 6 oz / ¾ cup orange lentils
1 x 400 g can chopped tomatoes
1.5 l / 3 pints / 6⅓ cups chicken
OR vegetable stock

salt and pepper
2 tbsp hazelnuts, lightly crushed
½ bunch flat leaf parsley, roughly chopped

METHOD

Heat the olive oil in a large pan and sweat the onion, carrots and celery until soft.

Add the garlic, cook for 2 minutes, then add the lentils.

Pour in the tomatoes and stock, bring to a boil, then reduce the heat and simmer for 1 hour until the lentils are completely soft.

Meanwhile lightly toast the hazelnuts in a dry frying pan or under a grill for a few seconds – watch them carefully.

If desired, whizz half the soup in a blender for a smoother texture, then return to the pan.

Season well and stir through the parsley before serving.

serves **4–6**

preparation time **10** mins

cooking time **1** hour

Courgette and Feta Omelette Brochettes

INGREDIENTS

1 tbsp butter
1 courgette (zucchini), finely diced
8 eggs
100 g / 3½ oz / ½ cup feta, crumbled
few sprigs mint, finely chopped
salt and pepper

METHOD

Heat the butter in a pan and when foaming, add a quarter of the courgette and cook gently until soft and translucent.

Meanwhile crack 2 eggs into a bowl and beat lightly. Tip into the pan and swirl gently to cover the base of the pan and help it set.

When the omelette is nearly set, sprinkle over a quarter of the feta, a little mint and seasoning and flash under a hot grill to set it completely. Remove from the pan, keep warm and set aside.

Repeat this process with the remaining ingredients, 2 eggs at a time, to make four omelettes.

Slice the omelettes into 3 equal slices, roll up and skewer through with a wooden kebab skewer.

Serve while still warm.

serves **4**

preparation time **5** mins

cooking time **20** mins

Noodle Vegetable Soup

INGREDIENTS

2 tbsp vegetable oil
1 onion, peeled and finely sliced
2 cloves of garlic, finely sliced
1cm piece fresh ginger, finely sliced
2 carrots, peeled and cut into matchsticks
1 courgette (zucchini), cut into matchsticks
1 red pepper, deseeded and finely sliced
1 yellow pepper, deseeded and
cut into matchsticks

1.5 l / 3 pints / 6⅓ cups chicken
OR vegetable stock

2 tbsp soy sauce
2 nests dried noodles
chilli sauce
salt and pepper
2 tbsp coriander, chopped

METHOD

Heat the oil in a large pan and sweat the onion until translucent.

Add the garlic and ginger and cook for 2 minutes, then add the remaining vegetables and cook for a few minutes.

Pour over the stock and soy sauce and simmer for 10 minutes.

Add the noodles and cook for about 5 minutes, until tender.

Adjust the seasoning and add the chilli sauce to taste.

Serve sprinkled with fresh coriander.

serves
4

preparation time
10 mins

cooking time
25 mins

Mussel and Potato Curry

INGREDIENTS

1 tbsp vegetable oil
1 onion, peeled and finely chopped
1 clove of garlic, finely chopped
1 large or 2 small sweet potatoes, peeled and diced

1 tbsp tamarind paste
pinch chilli flakes
2 tbsp fish sauce
1 x 400 g can coconut milk
100 ml / 3 ½ fl. oz / ½ cup chicken, fish **OR** vegetable stock

500 g / 1 lb/ 2 cups mussels, cleaned
juice of 1 lime and 1 lemon
salt and pepper

METHOD

Heat the oil in a large lidded pan and cook the onion and garlic until translucent.

Add the potatoes and cook for 5 minutes until just starting to soften.

Stir in the spices, then pour over the fish sauce, coconut milk and stock and simmer for 10-15 minutes until the potatoes are just tender.

Add the mussels, put the lid on and cook for 5-8 minutes until all the mussels are open. Discard any that remain closed.

Squeeze over the lime and lemon juice and adjust the seasoning before serving.

serves **4**

preparation time **10** mins

cooking time **35** mins

Chicken Caesar Salad

INGREDIENTS

2 chicken breasts, skinned
2 tbsp vegetable oil
4 rashers smoked streaky bacon
200 g / 7 oz / ¾ cup mixed salad leaves
100 g / 3½ oz / ½ cup ready–made croutons

For the dressing:
2 anchovy fillets
½ clove of garlic, crushed
150 ml / 5 fl. oz / ⅔ cup crème fraiche
squeeze of lemon juice
2 tbsp Parmesan, grated
salt and pepper

METHOD

Fry the chicken breast in a little oil, until cooked through. Thickly slice the chicken breasts and set aside.

Heat the oil in a pan and fry the bacon until crisp. Snip into small pieces and leave to drain on kitchen paper.

Tip the salad leaves into a large bowl and add the croutons.

For the dressing, mash the anchovy fillets with the garlic to a pulp, then stir in the crème fraiche, lemon juice and Parmesan and season carefully. You may want to add more lemon juice.

Add 2 tbsp of the dressing to the salad leaves and coat thoroughly.

Add the chicken and bacon to the salad then spoon over the remaining dressing.

serves 4

preparation time 15 mins

cooking time 5 mins

Vegetable Soup with Pasta

INGREDIENTS

3 tbsp olive oil
1 large onion, peeled and finely chopped
2 carrots, peeled and roughly chopped
2 sticks celery, chopped
1 clove of garlic, finely chopped
2 bay leaves
2 x 400 g can chopped tomatoes
1.5 l / 3 pints / 6⅓ cups vegetable stock
80 g / 2 ½ oz / ⅓ cup fusilli pasta
large handful green beans, topped & tailed
50 g / 1 ¾ oz / ¼ cup frozen peas
salt and pepper
extra virgin olive oil
Parmesan, to serve

METHOD

Heat the oil in a large pan and sweat the onion, carrot and celery until beginning to soften.

Add the garlic and bay leaves, cook for 3 minutes, then add the tomatoes and stock and bring to a simmer.

Add the pasta, cook for 5 minutes, then add the beans and peas and leave to simmer for another 6-7 minutes until all is tender. Season well.

This soup is best served a little warmer than room temperature with extra virgin olive oil drizzled over and a generous grating of Parmesan.

serves
4–6

preparation time
15 mins

cooking time
30 mins

Wild Rice and Vegetable Salad

INGREDIENTS

100 ml / 3 ½ fl. oz / ½ cup extra virgin olive oil
juice of 1 lemon
juice of 1 orange
½ bunch mint leaves
salt and pepper
250 g / 9 oz / 1 cup wild rice
100 g / 3½ oz / ½ cup soya beans, cooked
100 g / 3½ oz / ½ cup frozen peas, cooked
16 mixed cherry tomatoes, quartered
1 bunch spring onions (scallions), finely chopped
1 green eating apple, cored and diced
1 tbsp orange zest, finely grated

METHOD

Make the dressing by whisking together the oil, citrus juices, mint leaves and seasoning to make an emulsion.

Cook the wild rice in boiling water according to packet instructions. Drain and cover with half the dressing to allow the rice to soak up the flavours.

Toss together the soya beans, peas, tomatoes, spring onions and apple, then add to the rice and use a spoon to mix well.

Drizzle over more dressing, a sprinkling of fresh mint leaves and grated orange zest before serving.

serves
4

preparation time
20
mins

cooking time
25
mins

Salt Cod and Cream Frittata

INGREDIENTS

500 g / 1 lb salt cod, soaked overnight and rinsed thoroughly many times

500 ml / 1 pint / 2 cups milk

500 g / 1lb / 2 cups new potatoes, cooked, cooled and cubed

4 tbsp olive oil

½ bunch parsley, chopped

6 eggs, lightly beaten

salt and pepper

100 ml / 3½ fl oz / ½ cup double (heavy) cream

METHOD

Place the cod in a pan and cover with the milk. Bring slowly to the boil, then reduce the heat and cook for about 12 minutes or until the fish is cooked through and tender.

Drain and flake the fish into a bowl, discarding any skin and bones.

Heat the oil in a large frying pan and add the potatoes. Cook for a few minutes to give them a slightly golden crust, then stir in the fish and parsley.

Season the eggs, then pour into the pan. Swirl the pan to move the eggs into all the corners and coat everything.

Pour in the cream, a little at a time, so it forms small pools in the eggs.

Place under a hot grill for about 5-6 minutes to set the frittata – keep checking it to ensure nothing burns.

Allow to cool a little then cut into wedges and serve.

serves **4**

preparation time **20** mins

cooking time **30** mins

Potato, Fennel and Herb Frittata

INGREDIENTS

500 g / 1lb new potatoes
4 tbsp olive oil
1 fennel bulb, peeled and finely chopped, fronds reserved
1 bunch dill, chopped
½ bunch parsley, chopped
6 eggs, lightly beaten
salt and pepper

METHOD

Cook the potatoes in boiling salted water until tender to the point of a knife. Drain and set aside to cool. When cool, cut into quarters.

Heat the oil in a large frying pan and cook the fennel until tender.

Add the potatoes and cook for a few minutes to give them a slightly golden crust, then stir in the herbs.

Season the eggs, then pour into the pan. Swirl the pan to move the eggs into all the corners and coat everything.

Place under a hot grill for about 5-6 minutes to set the frittata – keep checking it to ensure nothing burns.

Allow to cool a little then cut into wedges, sprinkle with the fennel fronds and serve.

serves **4**

preparation time **10** mins

cooking time **30** mins

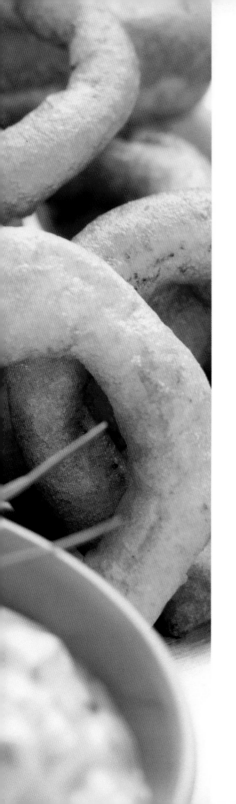

Starters & Sides

Fried Herby Cheese Cubes

INGREDIENTS

200 g / 7 oz / ¾ cup breadcrumbs
1 tbsp thyme leaves
1 tsp mustard powder
pinch cayenne pepper
salt
250 g / 9 oz / 1 cup cheese
2 eggs, beaten
vegetable oil

METHOD

Place the breadcrumbs in a food processor with the thyme leaves, mustard powder, cayenne and salt and whizz until everything is finely chopped and combined.

Cut the cheese into bite-size cubes.

Using a toothpick to spear the cheese cubes, dip into the egg and then the breadcrumbs, coating thoroughly.

Heat 1cm depth of oil in a large pan and when it sizzles when a few breadcrumbs are dropped in, add the cheese cubes in batches.

Cook until crisp and golden on all sides, removing to kitchen paper when done.

Serve hot with tomato salsa for dipping.

serves
6

preparation time
15
mins

cooking time
15
mins

Pan-fried Beans with Peppers

INGREDIENTS

100 g / 3½ oz / ½ cup green beans, topped and tailed

2 tbsp olive oil
1 red pepper, deseeded and finely sliced
½ bunch spring onions (scallions), finely chopped
juice of 1 lemon
salt and pepper

METHOD

Parboil the beans for 4 minutes in salted water until just tender, then plunge into iced water to stop the cooking and retain the colour.

Heat the oil in a pan until quite hot, then add the peppers and cook until tender and lightly golden in patches.

Add the beans and spring onions, toss to warm through, then add the lemon juice and season.

Serve immediately.

serves **2**

preparation time **5** mins

cooking time **10** mins

Mushroom Cous Cous

INGREDIENTS

250 g / 9 oz / 1 cup cous cous
2 tbsp sultanas
250 ml / 9 fl. oz / 1 cup chicken
OR vegetable stock

squeeze of lemon juice
2 tbsp olive oil
100 g / 3 ½ oz / ½ cup mushrooms,
thickly sliced

1 clove of garlic, crushed
½ red pepper, deseeded and finely chopped

½ green pepper, deseeded and
finely chopped

½ yellow pepper, deseeded and
finely chopped

salt and pepper
½ bunch parsley, roughly chopped
1 small courgette (zucchini), finely chopped
1 tbsp fresh thyme, chopped
thyme sprigs to garnish

METHOD

Place the cous cous in a bowl, cover with the hot stock and clingfilm the bowl. Leave for 10 minutes or so until tender, then fork through the grains and add the lemon.

Meanwhile heat the oil in a pan and sauté the mushrooms until golden in patches and any excess moisture has evaporated.

Add the garlic, courgette and diced peppers and toss to coat and cook for 3 minutes.

Tip the sautéed vegetables into the cous cous.

Season generously then add the parsley, garnish with sprigs of thyme and serve.

serves
4

preparation time
10
mins

cooking time
6
mins

Thyme-Marinated Mushrooms

INGREDIENTS

4 tbsp olive oil

250 g / 9 oz / 1 cup mixed mushrooms, thickly sliced

2 cloves of garlic, finely chopped

3 tbsp thyme leaves

200 ml / 7 fl. oz / ¾ cup red **OR** white wine vinegar

salt and pepper

METHOD

Heat the oil in a pan and sauté the mushrooms until golden in patches and any excess moisture has evaporated.

Add the garlic and thyme and season, toss to coat.

Pour in the vinegar and bring to a bubble, then simmer for a few minutes to reduce.

Pour into a bowl, leave to cool, then refrigerate until needed.

Serve as part of a salad or alongside steak.

makes
4

preparation time
5 mins

cooking time
10 mins

Onion Rings

INGREDIENTS

1 large Spanish onion, peeled
200 ml / 7 fl. oz / ¾ cup buttermilk
150 g / 5 oz / ⅔ cup plain
(all–purpose) flour

1 tsp baking powder
½ tsp bicarbonate of soda
pinch cayenne pepper
1 tsp mustard powder
vegetable oil

For the tartare sauce:
200 g / 7 oz / ¾ cup mayonnaise
2 tbsp capers, chopped
2 gherkins (cornichons), finely chopped
1 bunch chives, finely chopped
juice of ½ lemon
salt and pepper

METHOD

Cut the onion into rings so you end up with as many large onion rings as you can and discard any leftovers or keep for later cooking.

Separate the rings out then place in a bowl and macerate them in the buttermilk for 4 hours or overnight.

Mix together the flour, baking powder, bicarbonate of soda and spices.

Shake off any excess buttermilk from the onion rings and dip into the flour, coating thoroughly.

Leave them to dry for 10 minutes, then repeat the process so they have a thick floury coating.

Heat the vegetable oil until a bread cube sizzles immediately when dropped in, then fry the onion rings in batches, turning them over half way through cooking. Remove to kitchen paper to drain before serving.

Make the tartare sauce by mixing together all the ingredients. Serve alongside the onion rings.

makes **2–4**

preparation time **20** mins

cooking time **10** mins

Potato and Sausage Salad

INGREDIENTS

500 g / 1 lb / 2 cups new potatoes
2 tbsp vegetable oil
4 Frankfurters or sausages
1 tbsp Dijon mustard
2 tbsp red wine vinegar
salt and pepper
4 tbsp extra virgin olive oil
4 gherkins (cornichons), finely diced
2 tbsp fresh chives, chopped

METHOD

Cook the potatoes in boiling salted water until tender to the point of a knife.

Meanwhile heat the oil in a pan and fry the sausages until golden and sticky and cooked through.

Whisk together the mustard, vinegar and seasoning, then whisk in the oil to make an emulsion.

Drain the potatoes, then while still hot slice thickly. Toss in the mustard dressing so they soak up the flavours.

Cut the sausage into thick slices at an angle and add to the potatoes.

Serve hot, garnished with the chopped gherkins, a sprinkling of salt and pepper and garnish with chopped chives.

serves **4**

preparation time **5** mins

cooking time **20** mins

Parsnip
and Potato Straws

INGREDIENTS

2 parsnips, peeled
1 large sweet potato, peeled
vegetable oil
salt

METHOD

Using a mandoline cut the parsnips and sweet potatoes into fine julienne. If you don't have a mandoline, cut them into as fine matchsticks as you can manage. You could even grate them, although they would be shorter.

Fill a saucepan a third full with vegetable oil and heat to 180°C / 350F or until a piece of parsnip sizzles when dropped in.

Fry the vegetable straws in batches, using a wire ladle to scoop them out when crisp and golden onto kitchen paper to drain.

Sprinkle with salt and serve.

serves **4**

preparation time **20** mins

cooking time **3** mins

Fried Potatoes with Rosemary

INGREDIENTS

4 large baking potatoes, cut into
thick wedges
4 tbsp olive oil
1 large sprig rosemary, leaves
finely chopped
2 cloves of garlic, crushed
salt and pepper

METHOD

Parboil the potato wedges in boiling salted water for 5 minutes until just starting to soften.

Drain and set back over the heat to drive off any excess water. Roughen up the edges a little to help them crisp in the pan.

Heat the oil in a large pan and add the parboiled wedges and seasoning, cover with a lid and cook for about 5 minutes until the underside is crisp and golden.

Add the rosemary and garlic and toss in the pan every few minutes until the wedges are crisp and golden.

serves
4

preparation time
5
mins

cooking time
30
mins

Mains

Pesto Tagliatelle

INGREDIENTS

2 handfuls pine nuts, lightly toasted
1 clove of garlic, peeled and chopped
2 bunches basil
80 g / 3 oz / ⅓ cup Parmesan, grated
extra virgin olive oil
salt and pepper

320 g / 11 oz / 1 cup tagliatelle
Parmesan, to serve

METHOD

Whiz the ingredients for the pesto in a food processor to a rough paste, drizzling in enough olive oil to loosen.

Cook the pasta in boiling salted water according to packet instructions.

Drain, reserving a tbsp of the water.

Toss with the pesto and reserved water and serve immediately, sprinkled with more Parmesan.

serves	preparation time	cooking time
4	**5** mins	**11** mins

Jambalaya Chorizo

INGREDIENTS

2 tbsp olive oil
1 onion, peeled and finely sliced
2 cloves of garlic, finely chopped
2 stalks of celery, finely chopped
100 g / 4 oz / ⅓ cup chorizo
sausage, diced

1 chilli, deseeded and finely chopped
200 g / 7 oz / ¾ cup white basmati rice
600 ml / 1¼ pints / 2½ cups chicken stock
2 ripe tomatoes, chopped
50 g / 1 ¾ oz / ¼ cup frozen peas
12 raw large prawns, shells on
Tabasco sauce
juice of 1 lemon
salt and pepper

METHOD

Heat the oil in a pan and fry the onion, garlic and celery until golden.

Add the chorizo and fry until the fat starts to run, then add the chilli and rice and stir to coat thoroughly.

Pour over the stock, bring to a simmer, turn down the heat and leave to cook for about 15 minutes.

Stir in the tomatoes, peas and prawns and cook until the prawns have turned completely pink.

Season with Tabasco sauce, lemon juice and salt and pepper before serving.

serves **4**

preparation time **10** mins

cooking time **30** mins

Chicken and Coconut Curry

INGREDIENTS

3 tbsp vegetable oil
1 onion, peeled and finely sliced
2 cloves of garlic, finely chopped
2 tbsp red Thai curry paste
3–4 chicken breasts, skinned and cubed
2 tsp tamarind paste
400 ml / 14 fl. oz / 1½ cups coconut milk
200 ml / 7 fl. oz / ¾ cup chicken stock
salt and pepper
juice of 1–2 limes

boiled rice, to serve

METHOD

Heat the oil in a wok or large pan and fry the onion until deep gold and sweet.

Add the garlic and curry paste and cook out for 2 minutes.

Add the cubed chicken and allow to colour on all sides.

Stir in the tamarind, then pour over the coconut milk and chicken stock.

Lower the heat and leave to simmer for 15-20 minutes until the chicken is cooked through.

Adjust the seasoning and stir in the lime juice just before serving with boiled rice.

serves **4**

preparation time **15** mins

cooking time **30** mins

Linguine with Tomato

INGREDIENTS

160 g / 5 oz / ⅔ cup linguine
1 tbsp butter
1 red onion, peeled and finely chopped
2 ripe tomatoes, chopped
1 sprig thyme leaves
1 x 400 g can cannellini or flageolet beans, drained
250 ml / 9 fl. oz / 1 cup oat cream or double (heavy) cream

salt and pepper
1 tbsp chopped flat leaf parsley

METHOD

Cook the linguine in boiling salted water according to packet instructions.

Heat the butter in a pan and sweat the onion without colouring until tender.

Add the tomatoes, beans and thyme and heat through.

Drain the pasta, retaining a little of the cooking water, then set aside.

Add the cream to the sauce with a little pasta water to lubricate, then season.

Tip in the linguine and toss until coated, garnish with the chopped parsley then serve.

serves
2

preparation time
10 mins

cooking time
12 mins

Tuscan Lemon Chilli Chicken

INGREDIENTS

3 tbsp olive oil
4 chicken breasts, skin on
2 lemons, thinly sliced
2 onions, peeled and cut into eighths
1 red chilli, deseeded and finely sliced
2 cloves of garlic, finely sliced
200 ml / 7 fl. oz / ¾ cup chicken stock
salt and pepper
1 bunch sorrel, chopped

METHOD

Heat the olive oil in a large lidded pan and sear the chicken, skin side down until golden and crisp. Turn over and cook for 2 minutes on the other side, then remove from the pan and set aside.

Add the lemon slices to the pan and sear on either side until golden – a few seconds. Remove and set aside.

Add the onions and repeat, cooking until golden and caramelised.

Add the chicken back to the pan with the lemons, then add the chilli, garlic and stock, season and add the lid.

Cook over a low heat for 10-15 minutes until the chicken is just cooked through.

Add the chopped sorrel, adjust the seasoning and serve.

serves **4**

preparation time **10** mins

cooking time **40** mins

Chilli con Carne

INGREDIENTS

2 tbsp vegetable oil
500 g / 1 lb / 2 full cups minced beef
1 onion, peeled and chopped
2 cloves of garlic, finely chopped
1 tsp paprika
1 tsp ground cumin

½ – 1 tsp cayenne pepper
OR ½ tsp dried chilli flakes

1 x 400 g can kidney beans
1 x 400 g can chopped tomatoes
300 ml / 10 fl. oz / 1 ¼ cups beef stock
20 g / ½ oz dark chocolate, finely chopped
salt and pepper

To serve:
juice of 1 lime
sour cream
boiled rice

METHOD

Heat the oil in a large casserole and cook the beef until browned.

Add the onion and garlic and fry for a further 5 minutes until golden.

Add the spices and mix well, then pour over the kidney beans, tomatoes and stock and bring to the boil.

Simmer over a low heat for at least 45 minutes, stirring occasionally, until the chilli has thickened and reduced.

When cooked to your liking, stir in the chocolate and season.

Serve with a squeeze of lime juice, sour cream and rice.

serves **4**

preparation time **5** mins

cooking time **60** mins

Pan-fried Sea Bass

INGREDIENTS

2 x 400 g can cannellini beans, drained
300 ml / 10 fl. oz / 1¼ cups chicken stock
1 sprig rosemary
1 clove of garlic, lightly squashed
100 g / 3 ½ oz / ¼ cup frozen peas
salt and pepper
50 g / 1¼ oz / ¼ cup butter, softened
1 bunch parsley, finely chopped
juice of 1 lemon

4 sea bass fillets, boned, skin on
2 tbsp olive oil

METHOD

Add the beans to a pan and cover with the chicken stock, garlic and rosemary. Bring to the boil and then simmer for 5 minutes.

Add the peas, season and simmer until the liquor has thickened and the peas are cooked.

Mash the butter with the parsley, a little seasoning and a squeeze of lemon juice. Refrigerate.

Meanwhile heat the oil in a frying pan and lay the sea bass fillets in, skin side down.

Cook for about 4 minutes until the skin is crisp, then carefully turn over with a spatula and cook the other side for 1 minute.

Remove to a plate and place rounds of the flavoured butter on top. Add the beans and peas and serve.

serves
4

preparation time
10
mins

cooking time
15
mins

Pasta with Meatballs

INGREDIENTS

For the meatballs:
400 g / 14 oz / 1 ½ cups minced beef
1 egg
2 tbsp parsley, chopped
1 clove of garlic, crushed
salt and pepper
1 thick slice of white bread, crusts removed
soaked in 2 tbsp milk

3 tbsp olive oil
1 x 400 g can chopped tomatoes or passata
400 ml / 14 fl. oz / 1 ½ cups beef stock
1 tsp sugar

350 g / 12 oz / 1⅓ cups spaghetti
Parmesan, grated to serve
sprigs of basil, to garnish

METHOD

Place the meat in a large bowl with the egg, garlic and 1 tbsp parsley and season.

Mulch the bread in your fingers and crumble into the mix. Mix everything together with your hands to become smooth and sticky.

Roll into small walnut-sized balls with cold wet hands, place on a tray and chill for 30 minutes.

Heat the oil in a pan and fry the meatballs in batches until brown.

Add the passata and stock, then add the sugar and season and bring to the boil. Lower the heat and simmer for about 20 minutes.

Meanwhile cook the pasta in boiling salted water according to packet instructions.

Drain and tip into a large bowl. Pour the sauce over the pasta, sprinkle over the parsley and Parmesan, garnish with sprigs of basil and serve.

serves
2–4

preparation time
20 mins

cooking time
30 mins

Griddled Steak

INGREDIENTS

2 x sirloin or ribeye steaks, about
3cm / 1 inch thick

olive oil
salt and pepper
2 sprigs rosemary
2 cloves of garlic, lightly crushed
juice of ½ lemon

METHOD

Rub the steaks all over with olive oil and season, then place in a dish with the rosemary and garlic. Cover and leave for 30 minutes.

Preheat a griddle pan or the barbecue until searingly hot.

Place the steaks in the pan, placing them away from you and leave for 2 minutes until char marks form.

Turn the steaks over and leave for 3 minutes.

At this point, for rare steak, you can remove them from the heat. If you prefer your beef more well cooked, turn the steaks once more and leave for another minute.

Wrap the steaks securely in a large piece of foil and leave to rest for at least 5 minutes, but no longer than 8.

Just before serving, squeeze over the lemon juice, season again and pour the juices back over the steaks on the plate.

serves
2

preparation time
30
mins

cooking time
5
mins

Ratatouille

INGREDIENTS

4–6 tbsp olive oil
2 onions, peeled and finely sliced
2 aubergines (eggplants), cut in half
lengthways and finely sliced
3 courgettes (zucchini), cut in half lengthways
and finely sliced
2 garlic cloves, finely chopped
3 red peppers, seeded and cut into strips
1 x 400 g can chopped tomatoes
1 tsp coriander seeds, crushed
salt and pepper
handful fresh basil leaves

METHOD

Heat the oil in a pan and cook the onions until deep gold and sweet.

Add the aubergines and cook for 2 minutes, then add the courgettes and garlic and cook for 2 minutes, then add the peppers and cook for 5 minutes.

Add the tomatoes and coriander seeds and leave to simmer for at least 30 minutes over a very low heat, stirring occasionally, until the vegetables are very soft.

Season and sprinkle over the basil before serving.

serves **4**

preparation time **10** mins

cooking time **50** mins

Vegetable Stroganoff

INGREDIENTS

1 head broccoli, cut into florets
200 g / 7 oz / ¾ cup green beans, topped and tailed

2 tbsp olive oil
1 onion, peeled and finely chopped
1 clove of garlic, finely chopped
1 red pepper, deseeded and finely sliced
1 yellow pepper, deseeded and finely sliced
1 tsp ground coriander
100 ml / 3½ fl. oz / ½ cup vegetable stock
300 ml / 10 fl. oz / 1¼ cup sour cream
1 tbsp paprika
salt and pepper

METHOD

Parboil the broccoli florets and green beans in salted water for 4 minutes until just cooked. Drain and set aside.

Heat the oil in a pan and add the onion. Cook until golden and tender.

Add the garlic and peppers and cook until just tender and starting to turn golden, then stir in the coriander.

Add the broccoli and beans into the pan, then add the stock and sour cream with paprika, stir well and leave to simmer for 5 minutes until slightly thickened.

Season well and serve with rice.

serves
4

preparation time
10
mins

cooking time
18
mins

Barbecue Chicken

INGREDIENTS
1 chicken jointed or 6 chicken legs

For the marinade:
2 tbsp olive oil
4 tbsp white wine vinegar
3–4 tbsp soy sauce
2–3 tbsp tomato ketchup
1 tbsp soft brown sugar
1 tsp mustard powder
1 tsp paprika
salt and pepper

METHOD
Pat the chicken dry and place in a large freezer bag.

Mix together the marinade ingredients and taste. You may want it sweeter, hotter or saltier so just keep adding and tasting.

Pour the marinade into the freezer bag and mulch together so the chicken is completely coated.

Refrigerate for at least 30 minutes.

Heat the barbecue until the coals are glowing and there are no flames while the chicken is coming to room temperature out of the fridge.

Cook on the barbecue, turning frequently for 25-35 minute until cooked through with no pink juices.

Leave to rest for 10 minutes then serve with a squeeze of lemon and barbecued vegetables.

serves **4–6**

preparation time **5** mins

cooking time **20** mins

Fajitas

INGREDIENTS

4 tbsp olive oil
1 onion, peeled and finely sliced
1 red pepper, deseeded and finely sliced
1 yellow pepper, deseeded and finely sliced

2 chicken breasts, skinned and thinly sliced
OR 2 rump steaks, thinly sliced
OR 2 lamb leg steaks, thinly sliced

1 tsp paprika
1 tsp ground cumin
1 tsp ground coriander
pinch dried chilli flakes
salt and pepper

8 tortilla wraps
sour cream
tomato salsa
guacamole

METHOD

Heat half the oil in a pan until nearly smoking, then cook the onion and peppers until golden and tender. Remove from the pan, keep warm and set aside.

Add the remaining oil and reheat, then add the meat and sprinkle over the spices.

Stir briskly for a 2-3 minutes until either the chicken is just cooked through or the lamb or beef is still pink in the centre. Remove and keep warm.

Wipe out the pan and use to warm the tortillas through.

Serve the vegetables with the meat, tortilla wraps and sauces.

serves
2–4

preparation time
10
mins

cooking time
10
mins

Herby Chicken Burgers

INGREDIENTS

500 g / 1 lb / 2 cups minced chicken
OR turkey
2 tbsp oil for cooking
1 bunch basil leaves, finely chopped
1 tsp Espelette pepper
salt
zest of 1 lemon
1 egg, beaten

METHOD

Mix the chicken with the basil, pepper, salt and lemon zest until thoroughly mixed.

Pour in enough beaten egg to bind, but don't let the mixture get too wet.

With wet hands, form the mixture into 8 small or 4 large burgers.

Chill in the refrigerator for 30 minutes.

Cook in a little oil for 3–4 minutes per side, depending on thickness.

serves
4

preparation time
10 mins

cooking time
10 mins

Tofu and Vegetable Noodles

INGREDIENTS

2 tbsp vegetable oil
½ onion, peeled and finely sliced
1 clove of garlic, finely sliced
1cm piece fresh ginger, finely sliced
1 red pepper, deseeded and finely sliced
1 yellow pepper, deseeded and finely sliced
handful of trimmed and sliced green beans
100 g / 3½ oz / ½ cup tofu, cubed
3-4 tbsp soy sauce
2 tbsp oyster sauce
1 tbsp chilli sauce
2 nests noodles
1 tbsp sesame oil
1 tbsp Szechuan peppercorns, crushed
2 tbsp pine nuts

METHOD

Heat the oil in a wok until nearly smoking then stir fry the onion, ginger and garlic until golden.

Add the vegetables and stir fry until just tender, then add the tofu and heat through.

Meanwhile cook the noodles in boiling salted water according to packet instructions, then drain.

Add the sauces to the pan and bubble up, then add the noodles and sesame oil.

Serve topped with the crushed peppercorns.

serves
2

preparation time
10 mins

cooking time
10 mins

Trout Wrapped in Bacon

INGREDIENTS

2 trout, cleaned
½ bunch sage leaves
50 g / 2 oz butter
1 lemon, sliced
8 slices streaky bacon
salt and pepper

METHOD

Open the trout up and place 2 sage leaves, a slice of lemon and 1 tsp of butter inside. Season well. Wrap 4 slices of bacon around each trout.

Heat a large pan over a medium heat with a little oil and pan fry the trout, around 5-6 minutes each side until the bacon is crisp and the flesh pulls away easily from the bone.

Serve with simply boiled buttered potatoes.

serves
4

preparation time
10 mins

cooking time
20 mins

Pork Stir-Fry

INGREDIENTS

2 tbsp vegetable oil
350 g pork fillet or belly
1 onion, peeled and finely sliced
½ pak choi (Chinese cabbage) shredded
2 cloves of garlic, finely sliced
1 tsp fresh ginger, grated
1 red pepper, deseeded and finely sliced
1 yellow pepper, deseeded and finely sliced
1 can bamboo shoots
1 handful beansprouts
75–100 ml / 2½–3½ fl. oz / ⅓–½ cup soy sauce
2–3 tbsp oyster sauce
2–3 tbsp sweet chilli sauce
salt and pepper

boiled rice or noodles, to serve

METHOD

Heat the oil in a wok until nearly smoking, then add the pork. Stir fry over a high heat until golden all over and the fat crisp. Remove from the pan with a slotted spoon.

Add the onion, garlic and ginger and stir fry for 2 minutes.

Add the vegetables and cook until crisp-tender.

Add the meat back to the pan and stir in the sauces.

Leave to bubble for a few minutes then check and adjust the seasoning if necessary.

Serve hot with the rice or noodles.

serves
4

preparation time
10 mins

cooking time
12 mins

Lemon Risotto

INGREDIENTS

2 tbsp olive oil
40 g / 1 oz butter
1 onion, peeled and finely chopped
1 celery stalk, peeled and finely sliced
320 g / 11 oz / 1⅓ cups risotto rice
100 ml / 3½ fl. oz / ½ cup dry white wine
1 L / 2 ¼ pints / 4 ¼ cups chicken
OR vegetable stock

salt and pepper
3 tbsp butter
zest and juice of 1–2 lemons
150 g / 5 oz / ⅔ cup Parmesan, grated

METHOD

Heat the oil and butter in a large pan and add the onion and celery. Cook until soft and translucent.

Add the rice and stir to coat in the butter.

Pour in the wine and stir the rice while the wine is absorbed.

Once the wine has cooked in, reduce the heat a little and add the hot stock, a ladleful at a time, stirring fairly continuously. This will give the risotto its creamy texture.

Keep stirring in the stock and tasting the rice. After about 15-20 minutes the rice should be soft but with a slight bite. If you've run out of stock before the rice is cooked, simply use water.

Season and remove from the heat. Add the butter, lemon zest and juice and Parmesan (mantecatura) and leave to melt into the risotto. Serve immediately.

serves **4**

preparation time **5** mins

cooking time **25** mins

Seafood Paella

INGREDIENTS

5 tbsp olive oil
1 onion, peeled and finely sliced
2 cloves of garlic, finely chopped
1 stalk celery, finely chopped
1 red pepper, seeded and sliced
350g / 12 oz / 1½ cups paella rice
2 pints chicken or vegetable stock
pinch saffron threads
1 tsp paprika
4 ripe tomatoes, chopped
50 g / 1¾ oz / ¼ cup frozen peas
12 raw prawns, shells on
24 mussels, cleaned

2 fillets chunky white fish, skinned, boned and cubed

4 small lobster claws
1 lemon
salt and pepper

METHOD

Heat the olive oil in a large shallow pan and cook the onion, garlic and celery until tender.

Add the pepper, cook for a further 5 minutes, then stir in the paella rice and coat thoroughly in the oil.

Stir the saffron into the stock then pour it over the rice. Add the paprika. Bring to a simmer and leave uncovered for 10 minutes.

Add the tomatoes, peas and seafood and cook for a further 8–10 minutes until everything is just cooked through and the mussels have opened.

Stir through the lemon juice, season well and serve.

serves **4**

preparation time **15** mins

cooking time **30** mins

Thai fried Rice

INGREDIENTS

1 tbsp vegetable oil
2 eggs, lightly beaten
1 tbsp soy sauce
½ onion, peeled and finely sliced
2 cloves of garlic, crushed
1 red chilli, deseeded and finely chopped
350 g / 12 oz / 1½ cups white rice, cooked and cooled
1 tbsp sesame oil
1 tbsp soy sauce
2 tbsp fish sauce
200 g / 7 oz / ¾ cup prawns, raw or cooked
2 chicken breasts, pre-cooked, sliced
salt and pepper
1 bunch coriander leaves, chopped
½ cucumber, finely sliced
1 lime, quartered

For the Prik Nam Pla:
2 cloves of garlic, finely sliced
1 red chilli, finely chopped
4–5 tbsp fish sauce

METHOD

Heat the oil in a wok till very hot, then add the eggs and the tbsp soy sauce and swirl to form a thin film on the wok.

When the eggs are cooked, move them to one side of the wok and add the onion, garlic and chilli and cook for a minute.

If using raw prawns, add them now and cook until pink.

Add the rice and coat thoroughly in all the ingredients, then add the sesame oil, soy and fish sauce and mix well.

Add the chicken (and cooked prawns if using) and toss until heated through.

Season, stir in the coriander and set aside briefly.

Mix together the ingredients for the dipping sauce in a small ramekin. Serve the Thai rice garnished with slices of cucumber and lime quarters.

serves
4

preparation time
20 mins

cooking time
10 mins

Desserts

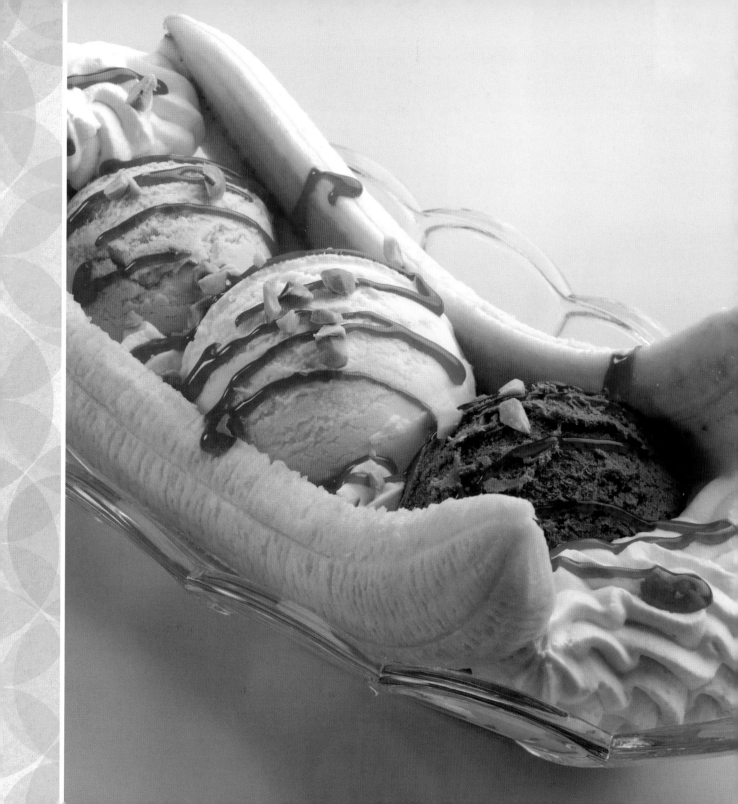

Banana Split

INGREDIENTS

200 ml / 7 fl. oz / ¾ cup whipping cream
1 tsp vanilla extract
4 bananas
4 scoops each good quality vanilla,
chocolate and strawberry ice cream
raspberry sauce, for serving
2 tbsp finely chopped hazelnuts

METHOD

Whisk the cream and vanilla extract into soft peaks then set aside.

Split the bananas in half and sandwich them around 3 scoops of ice cream.

Spoon the cream into a piping bag with a star nozzle and pipe around the bananas and ice cream.

Drizzle with raspberry sauce and sprinkle with chopped hazelnuts to serve.

serves
4

preparation time
10
mins

cooking time
0
mins

Orange Blossom Panna Cotta with Raspberry Coulis

INGREDIENTS

3 gelatine leaves, soaked in cold water
250 ml / 9 fl. oz / 1 cup milk
250 ml / 9 fl. oz / 1 cup double (heavy) cream

½ tsp orange blossom water
1½ tbsp caster (superfine) sugar

300 g / 10 oz / 1 ¼ cups raspberries
150 g / 5 oz / ⅔ cup icing (powdered) sugar
zest of 1 orange, finely grated

METHOD

Pour the milk, cream and orange blossom water into a pan with the sugar and simmer. Leave to infuse off the heat for 5 minutes.

Squeeze out the gelatine leaves, then stir into the pan until dissolved. Pour the mixture into 4 ramekins and leave to cool, then chill for at least 1 hour until completely set.

Meanwhile blitz the raspberries in a blender with the sugar to a smooth puree.

Pass through a sieve to remove any seeds.

Spoon the raspberry coulis onto the set panna cotta just before serving to create a smooth layer, then top with grated orange zest and serve.

serves
4

preparation time
15 mins

cooking time
2 mins

Sugar Cinnamon Doughnuts with Hot Chocolate Sauce

INGREDIENTS

8–12 ready-made small sugar doughnuts
1 tsp ground cinnamon

For the sauce:
200 g / 7 oz / ¾ cup dark chocolate
60 ml / 2 fl. oz / ¼ cup double (heavy) cream
1 tsp butter
1 tbsp golden syrup
pinch salt
pinch cayenne pepper (optional)
caster (superfine) sugar

METHOD

Place the doughnuts on a microwavable plate and sprinkle evenly with cinnamon. Warm in a microwave for 1 minute.

Melt the chocolate with the cream, butter and syrup in a bowl over simmering water until smooth and combined.

Remove from the heat and add the salt and cayenne pepper if using, then pour into a bowl.

Sprinkle the doughnuts with a little extra sugar before serving with the sauce.

serves
4

preparation time
10
mins

cooking time
1
mins

White Chocolate Raspberry Cheesecake

INGREDIENTS

100 g / 3½ oz / ½ cup digestive biscuits, crushed to crumbs

50 g / 1 ¾ oz / ¼ cup butter, melted
500 g / 1 lb / 2 cups white chocolate
60 g / 2 oz / ¼ cup butter
1 tsp vanilla extract
500 g / 1 lb / 2 cups cream cheese
2 tbsp caster (superfine) sugar
200 ml / 7 fl. oz / ¾ cup double (heavy) cream
200 g / 7 oz / ¾ cup raspberries

METHOD

Stir the biscuit crumbs into the melted butter and press into a greased 20cm loose-bottomed cake tin and chill to harden.

Melt the chocolate with the butter and vanilla extract in a bowl over simmering water. Remove and leave to cool slightly.

In a separate bowl, mix the cream cheese, sugar and cream until smooth.

Puree ¾ of the raspberries with a hand blender or mash them thoroughly with a fork.

Gently fold the chocolate mixture into the cream, then stir in the raspberry puree.

Spoon onto the biscuit base and chill for at least 12 hours before serving.

serves
8

preparation time
30 mins

cooking time
0 mins

Chocolate Mousse

INGREDIENTS

100 g / 3½ oz / ½ cup dark chocolate
1 tbsp water
2 eggs, separated
redcurrants, to garnish

METHOD

Melt the chocolate and tbsp water in a small bowl over a pan of simmering water.

Remove the melted chocolate from the heat, leave for 2 minutes, then beat in the egg yolks. Leave to cool for 10 minutes or so.

Meanwhile whisk the egg whites to soft peaks.

Fold the egg whites into the chocolate mixture using a metal spoon.

Spoon into individual glasses or a bowl, cover with clingfilm and chill for at least 6 hours.

serves
2

preparation time
20
mins

cooking time
3
mins

Crepe Suzette Purses

INGREDIENTS

125 g / 4 oz / ½ cup plain (all purpose) flour
pinch salt
1 egg
300 ml / 10 fl. oz / 1 ¼ cups milk
vegetable oil

juice of 4 oranges
zest of 1 orange
juice and zest of 1 lemon
1–2 tbsp caster (superfine) sugar
3–4 tbsp brandy liqueur
2 tbsp butter

METHOD

Tip the flour and salt into a bowl and make a well in the centre. Add the egg and beat into the flour.

Add the milk a little at a time until you have a smooth batter, then leave to stand for 20 minutes.

Heat a thin film of vegetable oil in a pan until very hot, then, using a ladle, line the pan with a thin film of batter and cook until bubbles come to the surface, then flip it. Cook on the other side for 2 minutes, then transfer to a warm place and repeat until all the batter is used up.

Fold the crepes into purses by gathering them together at the top and secure with a cocktail stick.

To make the sauce, mix together the citrus juices, zest and sugar.

Melt the butter in a pan, pour in the sauce and warm through.

Add the Grand Marnier and set light to it. Pour the flaming sauce over the pancakes so they are thoroughly soaked and serve.

serves **4**

preparation time **10** mins

cooking time **30** mins

Apricot and Blueberry Granita

INGREDIENTS

300 g apricots, stoned and chopped
100 g/3½ oz/ ½ cup sugar
200 ml/7 fl. oz/ ⅘ cup water

300 g blueberries
100 g /3 ½ oz/ ½ cup sugar
200 ml /7 fl. oz/ ⅘ cup water

METHOD

Cover the fruit with the sugar and water in separate pans and cook until soft enough to be mashed with a spoon.

Tip into a sieve and push through the sieve to leave a smooth sauce.

Pour the sauce into a freezer-proof container and freeze overnight.

Twenty minutes before serving, use a fork to scrape the granita into ice crystals, then serve layered in glasses with some fresh blueberries for decoration.

serves
4

preparation time
10
mins

cooking time
20
mins

Dark Chocolate Fondue

INGREDIENTS

400 g / 14 oz / 1½ cups dark chocolate
80 g / 2½ oz / ⅓ cup butter
400 ml / 14 fl. oz / 1½ cups double (heavy) cream
200 ml / 7 fl. oz / ¾ cup milk
1 tsp vanilla extract
1 tbsp honey
pinch salt
½ tsp ground cinnamon
pinch cayenne pepper

To serve:
mixed berries
brioche or slices of French toast
marshmallows

METHOD

Place the chocolate, butter, cream, milk, vanilla extract and honey in a saucepan over a very low heat and stir occasionally until melted and smooth.

Stir in the salt and spices.

Pour into a large bowl or a fondue bowl and dip the accompanying ingredients in. A tea light will also help keep the fondue warm.

serves **4–6**

preparation time **5** mins

cooking time **12** mins

Trifle

INGREDIENTS

400 ml / 14 fl. oz / 1½ cups ready-made custard

1 tsp vanilla extract
1-2 tbsp Framboise or any other fruit liqueur (optional)
400 g / 14 oz / 1½ cup raspberries
1 tbsp icing sugar
8 trifle sponges
2 tbsp grated chocolate, to garnish

METHOD

Mix the custard with the vanilla extract and fruit liqueur if using.

Lightly crush a third of the raspberries with the icing sugar to make a rough coulis.

Spoon a little custard into the bottom of 4 ramekins or glasses.

Place a sponge on top then drizzle over some coulis to soak in. Top with fresh raspberries. Spoon over some custard to cover, then repeat.

Top the trifles with fresh raspberries and a drizzle of coulis and refrigerate for 30 minutes before serving.

Garnish with grated chocolate.

serves
4

preparation time
10 mins

Strawberry Pudding

INGREDIENTS

100 g / 3½ oz / ½ cup strawberry jam
150 g / 5 oz / ⅔ cup butter, softened
150 g / 5 oz / ⅔ cup caster (superfine) sugar
zest and juice of 1 orange
3 eggs, lightly beaten
175 g / 6 oz / 1 cup self raising flour

100 g / 3 ½ oz / ½ cup strawberry jam
handful fresh strawberries

METHOD

Grease a 1.2L / 2 pint pudding basin and line the bottom with a circle of baking parchment.

Spoon the strawberry jam into the bottom of the basin and set aside.

Beat the butter, sugar and orange zest in a bowl until pale. Whisk in half the eggs, then half the flour, then repeat until everything is smooth.

Spoon into the pudding basin and level the surface with a palette knife. Either cover with a proper steaming lid or with pleated baking parchment and then foil, tied tightly under the rim with string.

Place an upturned saucer in a large deep pan and place the pudding basin on top. Add enough boiled water to come halfway up the sides, cover with a lid and steam for 90 minutes, checking frequently.

When a skewer inserted into the centre of the pudding comes out clean, the pudding is cooked. Remove from the pan and leave to stand.

Meanwhile heat the strawberry jam and fresh berries in a small pan with a little water so it is fairly liquid until the berries collapse a little.

Run a knife around the edge of the pudding basin to release it and turn it out onto a plate. Spoon the hot liquid strawberry sauce over the top and serve.

serves
4

preparation time
20 mins

cooking time
90 mins

Index

almonds, flaked
Muesli with Yoghurt, 21

anchovy fillets
Easy Chicken Caesar, 36

apple, eating
Baked Apples, 110
Wild Rice & Vegetable Salad, 40

apricots, dried
Apricot Blueberry Granita, 121
Muesli with Yoghurt, 21

aubergine
Ratatouille, 84

bacon
The Full English, 18
Easy Chicken Caesar, 36
Trout wrapped in Bacon, 96

baking powder
Onion Rings, 57

bamboo shoots, canned
Pork Stir-fry, 99

bananas
Banana Split, 109

basil, fresh
Herby Chicken Burgers, 92
Pasta Salad, 27
Pesto Tagliatelle, 67
Ratatouille, 84

bay leaves, fresh
Vegetable Soup with Pasta, 39

beans
Linguine with Tomato, 72
Pan-fried Sea Bass, 79
Chilli con Carne, 76
Wild Rice & Vegetable Salad, 40

beans, green
Pan-fried Beans with Peppers, 50
Vegetable Soup with Pasta, 39
Vegetable Stroganoff, 87

beansprouts
Pork Stir-fry, 99

beef
Chilli con Carne, 76
Pasta with meatballs, 80
Fajitas, 91
Griddled Steak, 83

bicarbonate of soda
Onion Rings, 57

biscuits, digestive
White Chocolate Raspberry
Cheesecake, 114

blueberries
Apricot Blueberry Granita, 121

branflakes
Muesli with Yoghurt, 21

bread
Dark Chocolate Fondue, 122
Poached Eggs and Ham on
Toasted Brioche, 10
Herby Scrambled Eggs, 14
The Full English, 18
French Toast with Chocolate, 13
Pasta with meatballs, 80
Fried Herby Cheese Cubes, 49

broccoli
Vegetable Stroganoff, 87

baking powder
Pancakes with Summer Berries, 17

berries, mixed
Dark Chocolate Fondue, 122
Pancakes with Summer Berries, 17

capers
Onion Rings, 57

carrots, fresh
Noodle Vegetable Soup, 32
Lentil Soup with Hazelnuts, 28
Vegetable Soup with Pasta, 39

cayenne pepper
Chilli con Carne, 76
Dark Chocolate Fondue, 122
Fried Herby Cheese Cubes, 49
Onion Rings, 57
Sugar Cinnamon Doughnuts with
Hot Chocolate Sauce, 113

celery, fresh
Jambalaya with Chorizo, 68
Lentil Soup with Hazelnuts, 28
Seafood Paella, 103
Simple Lemon Risotto, 100
Vegetable Soup with Pasta, 39

cheese
Fried Herby Cheese Cubes, 49
White Chocolate Raspberry
Cheesecake, 114
Courgette & Feta Omelette
Brochettes, 31
Cheese & Ham Croissant, 22
Fried Herby Cheese Cubes, 49
Fried Herby Cheese Cubes, 49
Easy Chicken Caesar, 36
Vegetable Soup with Pasta, 39
Pasta with meatballs, 80
Simple Lemon Risotto, 100

chicken, breasts
Chicken Caesar Salad, 36
Fajitas, 91
Thai-fried Rice, 104
Chicken & Coconut Curry, 71
Tuscan Lemon Chilli Chicken, 75
Herby Chicken Burgers, 92
Barbecue Chicken, 88

chocolate
Banana Split, 109
Chilli con Carne, 76
Chocolate Mousse, 117
Dark Chocolate Fondue, 122
Sugar Cinnamon Doughnuts with
Hot Chocolate Sauce, 113
White Chocolate Raspberry
Cheesecake, 114

chorizo sausage
Jambalaya with Chorizo, 68

chilli
Fajitas, 91
Mussel and Potato Curry, 35
Pasta Salad, 27
Chilli con Carne, 76
Jambalaya with Chorizo, 68
Thai-fried Rice, 104
Tuscan Lemon Chilli Chicken, 75
Noodle Vegetable Soup, 32
Pork Stir-fry, 99
Tofu and Vegetable Noodles, 95

cinnamon, ground
Baked Apples, 110
Dark Chocolate Fondue, 122
French Toast with Chocolate, 13
Sugar Cinnamon Doughnuts with
Hot Chocolate Sauce, 113

cod, salt
Salt Cod & Cream Frittata, 43

coconut milk
Mussel and Potato Curry, 35
Chicken & Coconut Curry, 71

coriander
Fajitas, 91
Vegetable Stroganoff, 87
Noodle Vegetable Soup, 32
Thai-fried Rice, 104
Ratatouille, 84

cous cous
Mushroom Cous Cous, 53

croissants
Cheese & Ham Croissant, 22

chervil, fresh
Herby Scrambled Eggs, 14

chives, fresh
Onion Rings, 57
Pesto Tagliatelle, 67
Poached Eggs and Ham on
Toasted Brioche, 10

crème fraiche
Chicken Caesar Salad, 36

courgette (zucchini)
Noodle Vegetable Soup, 32
Courgette & Feta Omelette
Brochettes, 31
Pasta Salad, 27
Ratatouille, 84
Tofu and Vegetable Noodles, 95

croutons
Chicken Caesar Salad, 36

cucumber
Thai-fried Rice, 104

cumin, ground
Chilli con Carne, 76
Fajitas, 91

custard, ready made
Trifle, 125

dill, fresh
Potato, Fennel & Herb Frittata, 44

doughnuts
Sugar Cinnamon Doughnuts with
Hot Chocolate Sauce, 113

dried fruit, mixed
Muesli with Yoghurt, 21

fennel, bulb
Potato, Fennel & Herb Frittata, 44

figs, dried
Muesli with Yoghurt, 21

fish, white
Seafood Paella, 103

fish sauce
Mussel and Potato Curry, 35
Thai-fried Rice, 104

framboise liqueur
Trifle, 125

gherkins (cornichons)
Potato & Sausage Salad, 58
Onion Rings, 57

ginger, fresh
Noodle Vegetable Soup, 32
Pork Stir-fry, 99
Tofu and Vegetable Noodles, 95

guacamole
Fajitas, 91

golden syrup
Sugar Cinnamon Doughnuts with
Hot Chocolate Sauce, 113

grand marnier
Crepe Suzette Purses, 118

ham
Cheese & Ham Croissant, 22
Poached Eggs and Ham on
Toasted Brioche, 10

hazelnuts, chopped
Lentil Soup with Hazelnuts, 28
Muesli with Yoghurt, 21

honey
Dark Chocolate Fondue, 122

ice cream
Banana Split, 109

jam, strawberry
Strawberry Pudding, 126

lamb, steaks
Fajitas, 91

lentils, dried orange
Lentil Soup with Hazelnuts, 28

lime, fresh
Chilli con Carne, 76
Mussel and Potato Curry, 35
Thai-fried Rice, 104
Chicken & Coconut Curry, 71

maple syrup
Pancakes with Summer Berries, 17
Porridge with Maple Syrup, 7

marshmallows
Dark Chocolate Fondue, 122

mayonnaise
Onion Rings, 57

mint, fresh
Pancakes with Summer Berries, 17
Pasta with meatballs, 80
Porridge with Maple Syrup, 7
Salt Cod & Cream Frittata, 43
Wild Rice & Vegetable Salad, 40

mushrooms, fresh
Mushroom Cous Cous, 53
The Full English, 18
Thyme-Marinated Mushrooms, 54

mustard
Potato & Sausage Salad, 58
Barbecue Chicken, 88
Fried Herby Cheese Cubes, 49
Onion Rings, 57

mussels, fresh
Mussel and Potato Curry, 35
Seafood Paella, 103

noodles, dried
Noodle Vegetable Soup, 32
Pork Stir-fry, 99
Tofu and Vegetable Noodles, 95

chocolate hazelnut spread
French Toast with Chocolate, 13

oat cream
Linguine with Tomato, 72

oatmeal, medium
Porridge with Maple Syrup, 7

orange, fresh
Baked Apples, 110
Crepe Suzette Purses, 118
Strawberry Pudding, 126
Wild Rice & Vegetable Salad, 40

oyster sauce
Pork Stir-fry, 99
Tofu and Vegetable Noodles, 95

paprika
Barbecue Chicken, 88
Chilli con Carne, 76
Fajitas, 91
Seafood Paella, 103
Vegetable Stroganoff, 87

parsnip
Parsnip & Potato Straws, 61

passata
Pasta with meatballs, 80

pasta
Pasta Salad, 27
Vegetable Soup with Pasta, 39

sausages
The Full English, 18
Potato & Sausage Salad, 58

Linguine with Tomato, 72
Pasta with meatballs, 80
Pesto Tagliatelle, 67

peas, frozen
Jambalaya with Chorizo, 68
Pan-fried sea bass, 79
Seafood Paella, 103
Vegetable Soup with Pasta, 39
Wild Rice & Vegetable Salad, 40

pepper
Herby Chicken Burgers, 92
Mushroom Cous Cous, 53
Noodle Vegetable Soup, 32
Fajitas, 91
Mushroom Cous Cous, 53
Pan-fried Beans with Peppers, 50
Pork Stir-fry, 99
Ratatouille, 84
Seafood Paella, 103
Tofu and Vegetable Noodles, 95
Vegetable Stroganoff, 87
Noodle Vegetable Soup, 32
Fajitas, 91
Mushroom Cous Cous, 53
Pork Stir-fry, 99
Tofu and Vegetable Noodles, 95
Vegetable Stroganoff, 87

pine nuts
Pesto Tagliatelle, 67

pork, belly
Pork Stir-fry, 99

porridge oats, jumbo
Muesli with Yoghurt, 21

potatoes
Fried Potatoes with Rosemary, 62
Potato & Sausage Salad, 58
Potato, Fennel & Herb Frittata, 44
Salt Cod & Cream Frittata, 43
Parsnip & Potato Straws, 61
Mussel and Potato Curry, 35

prawns
Jambalaya with Chorizo, 68
Seafood Paella, 103
Thai-fried Rice, 104

prunes
Muesli with Yoghurt, 21

pumpkin, seeds
Muesli with Yoghurt, 21

raspberries
White Chocolate Raspberry
Cheesecake, 114

rice
Chilli con Carne, 76
Pork Stir-fry, 99
Thai-fried Rice, 104
Chicken & Coconut Curry, 71
Seafood Paella, 103
Simple Lemon Risotto, 100
Jambalaya with Chorizo, 68
Wild Rice & Vegetable Salad, 40

rosemary, fresh
Fried Potatoes with Rosemary, 62
Griddled Steak, 83
Pan-fried sea bass, 79

rye flakes
Muesli with Yoghurt, 21

saffron, threads
Seafood Paella, 103

sage, leaves
Trout wrapped in Bacon, 96

salad leaves, mixed
Easy Chicken Caesar, 36

sausages
The Full English, 18
Potato & Sausage Salad, 58

sea bass
Pan-fried sea bass, 79

sorrel, fresh
Tuscan Lemon Chilli Chicken, 75

soy sauce
Barbecue Chicken, 88
Noodle Vegetable Soup, 32
Pork Stir-fry, 99
Thai-fried Rice, 104
Tofu and Vegetable Noodles, 95

strawberries, fresh
Strawberry Pudding, 126

sultanas
Mushroom Cous Cous, 53
Muesli with Yoghurt, 21

Tabasco
Jambalaya with Chorizo, 68

tamarind paste
Mussel and Potato Curry, 35
Chicken & Coconut Curry, 71

tarragon
Herby Scrambled Eggs, 14

thai curry paste, red
Chicken & Coconut Curry, 71

thyme, fresh
Fried Herby Cheese Cubes, 49
Thyme-Marinated Mushrooms, 54

tofu
Tofu and Vegetable Noodles, 95

tomatoes, canned chopped
Chilli con Carne, 76
Lentil Soup with Hazelnuts, 28
Pasta with meatballs, 80
Ratatouille, 84
Cheese & Ham Croissant, 22
Jambalaya with Chorizo, 68
Linguine with Tomato, 72
Seafood Paella, 103
The Full English, 18

tomatoes
Pasta Salad, 27
Wild Rice & Vegetable Salad, 40
Barbecue Chicken, 88
Fajitas, 91

trout
Trout wrapped in Bacon, 96

tuna, canned
Pasta Salad, 27
Vegetable Soup with Pasta, 39

turkey, minced
Herby Chicken Burgers, 92

vinegar, red wine
Potato & Sausage Salad, 58
Pasta Salad, 27
Thyme-Marinated Mushrooms, 54

vinegar, white wine
Barbecue Chicken, 88
Thyme-Marinated Mushrooms, 54

vanilla extract
Banana Split, 109
Dark Chocolate Fondue, 122
French Toast with Chocolate, 13
Pancakes with Summer Berries, 17
Trifle, 125
White Chocolate Raspberry
Cheesecake, 114

wine, white
Simple Lemon Risotto, 100

yoghurt
Muesli with Yoghurt, 21